Decoding French Wine: A Beginner's Guide to Enjoying the Fruits of the French Terroir

Andrew Cullen

Copyright © 2013 Andrew Cullen

All rights reserved.

ISBN: 1479303186
ISBN-13: 978-1479303182

"Give me books, French wine, fruit, fine weather and a little music played out of doors by somebody I do not know."

— *John Keats*

Table of Contents

Introduction

Overheard: "But the Label Doesn't Say Anything. Is this a Cab?"

Bordeaux

Left Bank Bordeaux Wines

Right Bank Bordeaux Wines

White Wines of Bordeaux

A String of Excellent Vintages in Bordeaux

Loire Valley

Burgundy (Bourgogne)

Cote d'Or

Beaujolais

Chablis

Alsace

Rhone Valley

Northern Rhone

Southern Rhone

Languedoc-Roussillon

Champagne

French wine tasting guide with suggested pairings

Decoding French Wine: A Beginner's Guide to Enjoying The Fruits of the French Terroir

Ten years ago, I was at a wine tasting that was dubbed a "Southern Hemisphere" wine tasting. Kind of a fun idea I thought. But what I took away from that night really had nothing to do with wines from Australia, South Africa and South America. Instead, it was an off the cuff conversation with the host, who was the South Eastern US rep for a large wine distribution company.

I shared with him the fact that I wanted to learn more about wine. Not only did I feel intimidated outside of the Cabernet aisle at my local store, but I had just been to a business dinner the prior week where an executive we were dining with started ordering wine by the name and year without opening the wine list. I was impressed, in a James Bond sort of way. It was the birth of what would become a mild obsession for me – to enjoy and understand the world of wine.

I began talking with the wine rep about my favorite wines at the tasting and other wines that I enjoyed. I told him that I had lived in the Northwest for eight years and had the opportunity to partake in what would become the strong emerging market for Pinots (and now Cabs and a whole bunch of awesome wines) from Washington and Oregon. And I expressed a love for Napa Cabs.

But I also had a burgeoning appreciation for wines from Europe and a couple of trips to France really kicked it off. I tried Pauillac Bordeaux; sampled plenty of Chateauneuf-du-papes, drank carafes of other Rhone wines in outdoor restaurants in Nice and found a fondness for Nuits-Saint-Georges and Chablis. I had developed a love for French wine, and I knew I was only in the opening innings of a long and exciting game.

So back to the night of the wine tasting – the wine rep told me that I should pick an area of Europe to focus on, and the two most notable ones were France and Italy (Spain after that, at least in terms of volume). Both he said would provide a lifelong journey into their wines and neither would be mastered easily. But by focusing on one, I would also be able to really get a grasp on what made that territory such a global wine powerhouse. And so began my journey into French wine.

Now for a quick disclaimer about this book. I am not trying to come across as an expert in French wine. I truly believe it is a lifelong journey and I am still learning as much now as I did ten years ago, and maybe even more now that I'm immersed. This book is not intended to be "the definitive guide" to French wine. Instead, it is geared toward that beginning consumer, that person who is interested in French wine, who wants to learn more about it, who wants to understand what varietals are produced in the various regions and who wants to experience how the varying landscapes in France produce these amazing wines.

Now disclaimer number two – I am only writing about regions that I am familiar with. I am going to skip what many experts would likely deem to be some notable areas of France because I am just not familiar enough with them to offer the kind of insight I would like to. (Hence, the prior "lifelong journey" comments.) I'll get there eventually. It just takes time, a dedication to trying new wines and a couple more trips over the pond.

When you are starting out, and the entire wine world feels like a foreign language, you will find plenty of books that dive deep into everything there is to know about wine, and they provide more information than the beginning wine drinker wants to consume or can retain. I heard from many friends and readers of a wine website that I run that these books are just too overwhelming. There's so much to learn and there are so many areas to cover.

So, let's focus, and look at key areas of the French wine landscape that will help get your journey into the world of wine in motion.

My Thoughts on Experiencing Wine

I also want to throw out what could be disclaimer number three, but really it's an idea that I see affecting more than just readers of this book. It affects the wine world at large.

Wine experiences are just that. They are experiences. How a particular wine hits you is how a particular wine hits *you*. Not anyone else. It's your experience. That's the beauty of it.

It's based on your own personal tastes but it's also based on your experience overall. It can be impacted by what you ate with the wine, or who you drank it with. It can be affected by your expectations for the wine, how much it cost or what someone told you that you should think. These circumstances are unavoidable and they play a crucial role in how you experience wine, and more importantly, how that wine, or that year, or that region, become logged into your memory.

I make a point to go at each wine I drink with as little bias as possible but it's almost impossible. There's usually some reason why a particular wine was purchased that will never go away. Recommendations from in store wine experts can make or break a wine for you. But so much involves individual tastes. If there's a wine you love for $10 and someone else thinks it's horrible, that's fine. If you drink a $100 bottle that scored 95 points from a wine expert and you think it's mediocre, that's fine too. It's individual. And your appreciation for certain wines may change over time as you try different bottles and your palate expands.

So as much as I write this trying to be neutral, it's impossible. So I will just say up front what I like.

Wines from France that I Love

There's no way around the fact that I love Bordeaux and Rhone bottles, particularly Chateauneuf-du-Pape. I prefer left bank Bordeaux over right bank, although I've had some killer right bank bottles recently that are beginning to sway me. For value under $25 I think the Rhone area of France (along with Languedoc) offers some of the best wines on the planet. And the Red Burgundy that I've had really impresses, particularly those from Nuits-Saint-Georges.

I've had many wines from Alsace, Loire, Burgundy, Bordeaux, Rhone, Languedoc, Champagne, Provence and everywhere in between. I have made my journey further into some regions than others, so far. This book will cover those that I have a better knowledge of based off of where I am in my journey. I would love to follow this book up with a second one that covers more. This particular story is French Wine by a guy who wants to help others experience and appreciate the French wine that he knows best.

Terroir:

1. A "terroir" is a group of vineyards (or even vines) from the same region, belonging to a specific appellation, and sharing the same type of soil, weather conditions, grapes and wine making savoir-faire, which contribute to give its specific personality to the wine.

2. A killer wine bar in the East Village of NYC

Overheard: "But the Label Doesn't Say Anything. Is this a Cab?"

As I stated before, my goal is to decode a French wine list for you, so you know what you are ordering and why. The French established a system a long time ago that designates certain regions, or appellations, throughout the country and the various appellations are under strict control as to what types of grapes and the quantity of those grapes that can be grown in those regions, which leads to what types of wines can be expected.

It's in vast contrast to how things are done in the US where you can get Cabernet Sauvignon focused wines from Paso Robles, or Napa, or Sonoma, or Washington, or even Arizona and Virginia. The French, in order to fight counterfeit wine production which ran rampant in the 19th century, and in an effort to always designate exactly what was being produced and where, made the distinction of naming their wines for the regions where they were grown rather than the grapes that make up the bottle.

It takes some time to get accustomed to this if you are entrenched in US wine consumption but after a little while exploring this system, it really does have some merit, and you also know exactly what you are getting. This system is common throughout Europe and really dictates why a wine education is such an extensive and ongoing practice. This is as much about geography as it is about anything else.

The first place we are going to stop is Bordeaux, which is not only where many world class wines are produced, but it is also where many of the most popular grape varietals originated from.

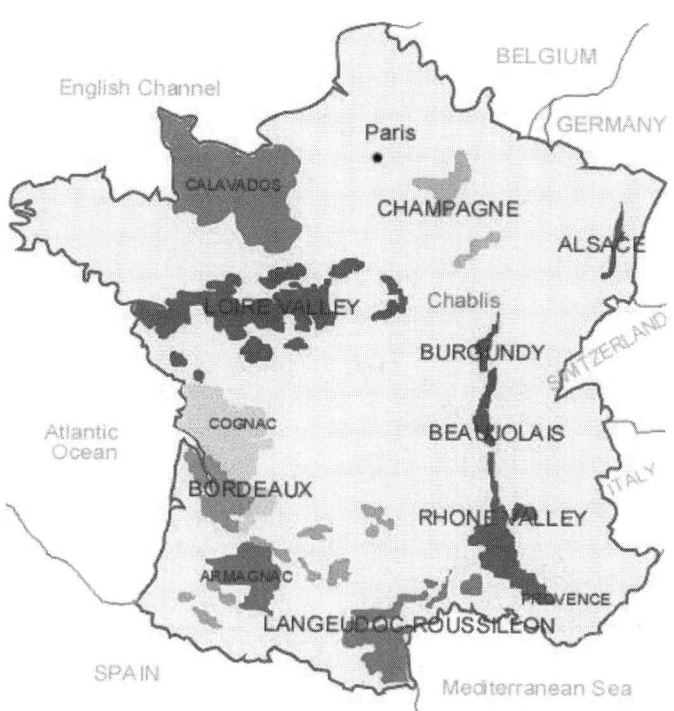

"French wines may be said but to pickle meat in the stomach, but this is the wine that digests, and doth not only breed good blood, but it nutrifieth also, being a glutinous substantial liquor; of this wine, if of any other, may be verified that merry induction: That good wine makes good blood, good blood causeth good humors, good humors cause good thoughts, good thoughts bring forth good works, good works carry a man to heaven, ergo, good wine carrieth a man to heaven."

- British writer James Howell (1634)

Bordeaux

Bordeaux is known for producing some of the most prized wines in the world, and with good reason. Just to be clear too, Bordeaux is a city in France. As I just stated, French wines will be labeled by city or appellation and then by specific areas within that appellation that tell you a little more about the wine and what to expect.

Bordeaux is divided into two main regions: left bank, meaning west of the Garonne river, and right bank, which is east of the river. While the two regions share the fact that they produce world class wines, the French have designated which grapes can grow in what quantity in each area. As a result you will get more Cabernet Sauvignon heavy wines on the left bank side and more Merlot based wines on the right bank side.

Remember that almost every wine produced in Bordeaux is a blend. There are 14 different grape varietals that are grown in Bordeaux and the main ones are Cabernet Sauvignon, Merlot, Cabernet Franc, Malbec and Petit Verdot. The French have become masterful at making wines this way, but to know what you're getting inside the bottle you have to pay attention to all the clues on the label, and be able to piece that together with your own knowledge, which hopefully is increasing (at least slightly I hope) as you are reading this.

Now you're probably wondering how to tell if a wine is a right bank or left bank? And it's not always obvious. Again you need to bring a little geographic research into the equation.

Left Bank Areas to Note

When you visit your local wine shop or look at French Bordeaux on a menu, you will want to note the year, the Chateau and the appellation within Bordeaux. Because you have studied the previous map, you will then be able to tell where the wine is from, what varietals it is likely made from and have an idea of what to expect.

The left bank of Bordeaux is legendary since all of the designated "First Growth" Bordeaux come from this area. More on that in a second.

Here are some of the top areas of the left bank to familiarize yourself with:

1. Margaux
2. St Julien
3. St Estephe
4. Pauillac
5. Medoc

Each of these areas exemplify the characteristics of what makes Bordeaux such an amazing place to grow wine, as evidenced by its several hundred year run at the top of the wine world. For this area, it's the perfect combination of gravelly soil (terroir), weather and history. Bordeaux grape vines are older and they've had time to crawl deep into the gravel and limestone to absorb the richness of this land. The climate is near perfect for wine growing, moderated by its close proximity to the Atlantic Ocean.

Because of these characteristics, Bordeaux wines will exhibit an "old worldness" to them; a little more of a rustic drink. In my opinion, it's what makes them special. It's what makes the French Merlot taste so good. It's the beauty and mastery of the blend, to harness all these great elements to produce a wine like no other.

The best way to experience this is to try different bottles from each of these areas. Try to find the same vintage so you can make a more direct comparison. On the more bargain priced side, look at the Medoc region (pronounced May Dock), specifically Haut-Medoc wines which are very good and can be found under $20. When you move into the Pauillac, St Julien, Margaux and St Estephe areas, the bottles can get much more expensive, especially those from good years (we'll cover some of the years soon since right now is a particularly good time to be buying Bordeaux).

While most of these left bank reds will be dominated by Cabernet Sauvignon, they will likely include smaller parts of Merlot, Cabernet

Franc and Petit Verdot. This mix is where we start to separate the left from the right.

Following is a list of the top rated Bordeaux producers by Chateau according to the Bordeaux Wine Official Classification of 1855. From First to Fifth growth, these are some names to commit to memory. Many of the First and Second growth wines on this list are among the most prized wines in the world.

First Growths (Premiers Crus)

Château Lafite Rothschild, Pauillac

Château Latour, Pauillac

Château Margaux, Margaux

Château Haut-Brion, Pessac, Graves

Château Mouton Rothschild, Pauillac

Second Growths (Deuxiémes Crus)

Château Rauzan-Ségla, Margaux

Château Rauzan-Gassies, Margaux

Château Léoville-Las Cases, St. Julien

Château Léoville-Poyferré, St. Julien

Château Léoville-Barton, St. Julien

Château Durfort-Vivens, Margaux

Château Gruaud-Larose, St. Julien

Château Lascombes, Margaux

Château Brane-Cantenac, Margaux

Château Pichon Longueville Baron, Pauillac

Château Pichon Longueville Comtesse de Lalande, Pauillac

Château Ducru-Beaucaillou, St. Julien

Château Cos d'Estournel, St. Estèphe

Château Montrose, St. Estèphe

Third Growths (Troisièmes Crus)

Château Kirwan, Cantenac-Margaux (Margaux)

Château d'Issan, Cantenac-Margaux (Margaux)

Lagrange, Château Lagrange, St. Julien

Château Langoa-Barton, St. Julien

Château Giscours, Labarde-Margaux (Margaux)

Château Malescot St. Exupéry, Margaux

Château Cantenac-Brown, Cantenac-Margaux (Margaux)

Château Boyd-Cantenac, Margaux

Château Palmer, Cantenac-Margaux (Margaux)

Château La Lagune, Ludon (Haut-Medoc)

Château Desmirail, Margaux

Château Dubignon, Margaux

Château Calon-Ségur, St. Estèphe

Château Ferrière, Margaux

Château Marquis d'Alesme Becker, Margaux

Fourth Growths (Quatrièmes Crus)

Château Saint-Pierre, St. Julien

Château Talbot, St. Julien

Château Branaire-Ducru, St. Julien

Château Duhart-Milon, Pauillac

Château Pouget, Cantenac-Margaux (Margaux)

Château La Tour Carnet, St.-Laurent (Haut-Médoc)

Château Lafon-Rochet, St. Estèphe

Château Beychevelle, St. Julien

Château Prieuré-Lichine, Cantenac-Margaux (Margaux)

Château Marquis de Terme, Margaux

Fifth Growths (Cinquièmes Crus)

Château Pontet-Canet, Pauillac

Château Batailley, Pauillac

Château Haut-Batailley, Pauillac

Château Grand-Puy-Lacoste, Pauillac

Château Grand-Puy-Ducasse, Pauillac

Château Lynch-Bages, Pauillac

Château Lynch-Moussas, Pauillac

Château Dauzac, Labarde (Margaux)

Château d'Armailhac, Pauillac

Château du Tertre, Arsac (Margaux)

Château Haut-Bages-Libéral, Pauillac

Château Pédesclaux, Pauillac

Château Belgrave, St.-Laurent (Haut-Médoc)

Château de Camensac, St.-Laurent (Haut-Médoc)

Château Cos Labory, St. Estèphe

Château Clerc-Milon, Pauillac

Château Croizet Bages, Pauillac

Château Cantemerle, Macau (Haut-Médoc)

Another Left Banker to Keep an Eye Out For

Graves is a left bank area on the southern portion of Bordeaux. Graves is noted for its Cabernet Sauvignon dominated red blends, and white wines blended from Sauvignon Blanc and Sémillon. Pessac-Leognan is a popular region within Graves that produces both red and white wines, and this is where the world famous Chateau Haut-Brion is located, so buying wines produced nearby is certainly not a bad idea. All the red blends I've tried from Pessac-Leognan have been winners, and you are starting to see more and more of them show up in US stores and on US restaurant lists.

In the southern part of Graves is another heavy hitting region called Sauternes, which is known for its white dessert wines. You will see some of the Sauternes bottles reach pretty high price points too, certainly higher than you'd expect for most dessert wines, and many of the finer wines produced in this region can age for a very long time. Luckily you also see them delivered in the smaller 375ml size, which is a good size for a sweet dessert wine.

Right Bank Areas to Note

Just because I pointed out that the left bank regions include all of the major first growth Bordeaux, don't count the right bank out at all. They produce some of the most exclusive, hard to find and expensive wines in the world. While the classification of 1855 designates the top "growth designated" wines for the left bank, the right bank has its own classification that was made in 1955.

Two huge right bank names to know are Chateau Petrus and Chateau Cheval Blanc, the latter of which was featured in its famous 1961 vintage as Miles' prized bottle of wine from the film Sideways.

These wines, along with other big guns like Chateau Pavie and Chateau Ausone, can fetch anywhere from a few thousand dollars a bottle to upwards of $30,000 a bottle depending on the year. So there is clearly something to be said about right bank wines, even if they are predominantly Merlot based, which Miles from Sideways ironically and famously dissed in the film.

Some key Right Bank Bordeaux areas to note include:

1. Pomerol

2. St Emilion

3. Fronsac

4. Bourg

5. Blaye

Here are the classifications for right bank Bordeaux under the 1955 formal classification in Saint-Émilion:

Premiers grands crus classés A

Château Ausone   Château Cheval Blanc

Premiers grands crus classés B

Château Angélus	Château Beauséjour (Duffau-Lagarrosse)	Château Beau-Séjour Bécot
Château Belair Monange	Château Canon Château Figeac	Clos Fourtet
Château La Gaffelière	Château Magdelaine	Château Pavie
Château Trotte Vieille	Château Troplong Mondot	

Grands crus classés

Château Balestard la Tonnelle	Château Bellevue	Château Bergat
Château Berliquet	Château Cadet Bon	Château Cadet Piola
Château Canon-la-Gaffelière	Château Cap de Mourlin	Château Chauvin
Château Corbin	Château Corbin Michotte	Château Dassault
Château Faurie de Souchard	Château Fonplégade	Château Fonroque
Château Franc Mayne	Château Grand Mayne	Château Grand Pontet
Château Guadet Saint-Julien	Château Haut Corbin	Château Haut Sarpe
Château L'Arrosée	Château La Clotte	Château La Couspaude
Château La Dominique	Château La Marzelle	Château La Serre

Château La Tour Figeac	Château La Tour du Pin Figeac (Giraud-Bélivier)	Château La Tour du Pin Figeac
Château Laniote	Château Larcis Ducasse	Château Larmande
Château Laroque	Château Laroze	Château Le Prieuré
Château Les Grandes Murailles	Château Matras	Château Moulin du Cadet
Château Pavie-Decesse	Château Pavie-Macquin	Château Petit Faurie de Soutard
Château Pipeau	Château Saint-Georges-Côte-Pavie	Château Soutard
Château Tertre Daugay	Château Villemaurine	Château Yon Figeac
Clos de l'Oratoire	Clos des Jacobins	Clos Saint-Martin
Couvent des Jacobins		

Fun side note: There is a French restaurant in New York City called Benoit (on West 55th) that serves high end French wines by the ounce. The bottles are stored in a special refrigerated preservation system that dispenses small amounts while keeping the rest of the bottle fresh. On a recent trip there they had 1988 Petrus by the ounce for $70. That is essentially one sip of wine for $70, but I had to do it. Petrus by the bottle can go for several thousand. And it was worth it. I thought it was an amazing wine, aged well with probably some time to run; a really great experience. I highly recommend checking Benoit out if you visit the city, and the food was beyond spectacular as well.

The White Wines of Bordeaux

Bordeaux is almost 90% dominated by red grape varietals, but the whites that come from this region shouldn't be discounted. Like the aforementioned Sauternes area and the famous Chateau d'Yquem, there are world class whites being produced here too.

White Bordeaux is predominantly made from Semillon and Sauvignon Blanc. For the everyday white Bordeaux you can find prices in the $10-$20 range and they are typically very good. In the US, the average consumer just doesn't go out in search of white Bordeaux so they can be harder to find and with a limited selection, but certainly no wine journey is complete without trying a few different bottles.

A String of Excellent Vintages in Bordeaux

Right now is an amazing time to be drinking Bordeaux wines. We have seen a string of incredible years that are in stores now, and the projections on the forthcoming vintages being assembled now are all very positive. But some years are better than others. And some get overlooked being right after a stellar year. So pay attention to the vintage. It will certainly dictate the price you pay but it will also correlate to the quality you receive.

Here are the top years for the past decade or so:

2000 (drinking wonderfully right now)

2003 (very good year)

2005 (legendary vintage. Cellarable. Highly desirable. I have a few on hand and have opened a couple recently. As of August 2013 (when I wrote this), I'd let them sit for a few more years. They still tasted young to me with room to run.)

2009 (strong year)

2010 (Maybe better than 2005. One of the best vintages in a long time. It's a good time to start scooping some of these up, before the price starts climbing as we saw happen very quickly with the buzz around the 2005. And with a very difficult year for Napa growers in 2011, I bet more of the wine drinkers in the know will move into these 2010 Bordeaux. Buy some good ones, and hold on to them.)

I constantly remind myself that when a vintage is gone, it's gone and can never come back. The 2005s (the good ones) are pretty much gone and the 2000s and 2003s are even harder to come by. If you see a Chateau you are interested in and can find one of these vintages or better yet a 2010, buy it. Also, if you find one of these vintages on a nice bottle at a restaurant, it should almost go without saying that you need to double-check the label when the wine is brought to the table. And make sure the server opens the bottle at the table. These are basic rules, but always very important, especially if you are enjoying yourself in good company and not paying close attention. I had a close call recently that I'm pretty sure was just an accident, but it's not a mistake that I ever want to pay for. A waiter brought out the wrong vintage and I didn't notice until the cork had been pulled. Luckily in this case I was at a nice steakhouse, and they had no problem going back and grabbing me the correct year. But not everyone will do that.

Loire Valley

The Loire Valley is located in the middle stretch of the Loire River in central France and it is home to several of France's major winegrowing areas including Muscadet, Sancerre and Pouilly-Fume.

Muscadet is made on the western end of the Loire Valley and is the major wine produced in Loire. The primary grape used is the Melon de Bourgogne, which is light in body and typically pretty dry, while remaining bright with crisp acidity. They are perfect with a range of seafood, and in my travels to France, it (along with Chablis) is a frequent go-to food wine.

Sancerre is perhaps the most popular and well known area of the Loire Valley and it has grown increasingly more visible in recent years in the US, perhaps because the wines are produced from Sauvignon Blanc, which US consumers tend to favor. Most of the Sauvignon Blancs are produced unoaked which really lets the richness and character of the stony soil take hold. They open up amazing and balanced citrus flavor, although not as forward as those from New Zealand, which for me, makes them more food friendly.

Pouilly-Fume, which is right next door, also produces Sauvignon Blanc based wines with similar characteristics. Like Sancerre these are becoming easier to find in most stores in the US in greater varieties. Pouilly-Fume whites are dry with mineral notes, and are also very food friendly. The "Fume" designation refers to the smoky nose frequently associated with these wines.

Burgundy (Bourgogne)

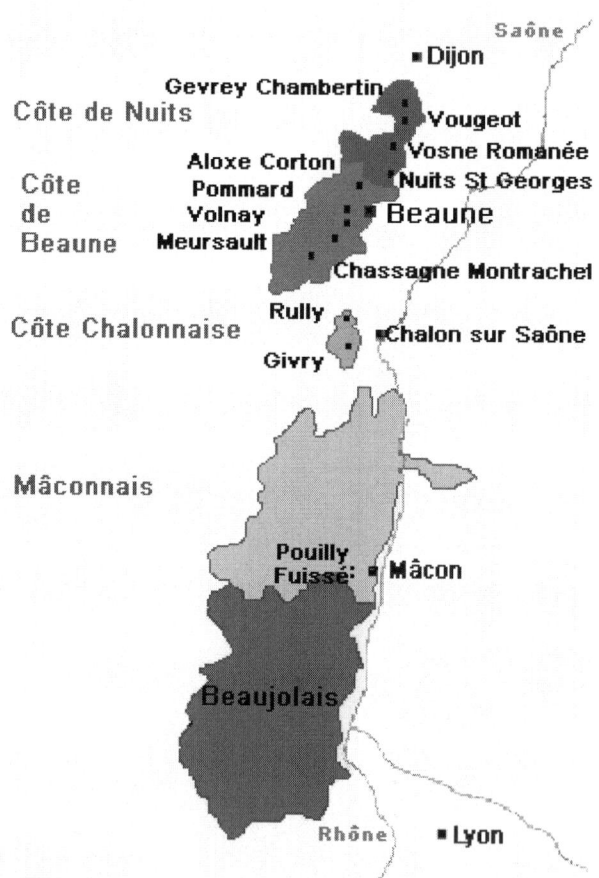

When you see a label or a bottle on a wine list that says Bourgogne, or Burgundy, you should instantly think Pinot Noir and Chardonnay, which are the two varietals you will see most commonly from this area. You may see signs in your store for Red Burgundy and White Burgundy, which makes this even easier to decode.

Burgundy is a large area with a ton of appellations throughout. Some of these areas are better known than others. In some areas, you will again find world class wines that demand a price tag into the thousands. In other areas, you can scoop up decent white burgundy for $20-$30. But overall, good Burgundy comes with a hefty price tag, compared to some of the other areas of France. And it is with good reason. The Pinot Noir grape is notoriously hard to grow, and really hard to master, particularly with the sometimes unpredictable weather in Burgundy. Luckily many of these French winemakers have been at this for some time, dating back generation after generation in their family. This deep history of wine making is something we are only beginning to establish in the US. Experience breeds knowledge.

Fast Fact: Burgundy has more than 400 types of soil that vineyards are planted in.

The wines of Burgundy taste a little different than the Pinot Noir you might be used to drinking from California, or Oregon. The French Pinot Noir again benefits from the amazing land and old vines, tasting a little more old world, dry and chalky compared to their US counterparts. There is layer after layer of complexity on the palate which only gets better as the wine gets some air. These are wines that age incredibly well, sometimes for decades in the case of the very best Burgundies.

Cote d'Or is a name to remember. Wines from Cote d'Or are legendary and known around the world for their fine quality and elegance. Now before you rush out to the store and find an off brand Cote d'Or bottle for $15 (because a few do exist), take a good look at this area, and make the effort to develop a good appreciation for what makes it so special.

Cote d'Or is divided into two regions, Cote de Nuits and Cote de Beaune. And then a number of subregions, such as Nuits-Saint-Georges, which is one of my favorites. The best way to explore this area is to always try something new. If you do, you will start to develop a taste for what you like and an understanding of how the areas differ from one another.

Beaujolais is an area of Burgundy that you might be familiar with given the incredible retail marketing effort for the release of these wines around Thanksgiving every year. Beaujolais is made from the Gamay grape, and in most incarnations is meant to be consumed young (often times in the year it's released). The cheap Beaujolais will taste really young and fresh, like it was bottled yesterday, and I'll admit it works ok for the Thanksgiving feast. But if you venture out a bit and try some of the Cru Beaujolais, they get quite good. I should thank the always knowledgeable folks at the Terroir wine bar in the east village of NYC for helping me gain that insight.

Chablis is a very important region of Burgundy and the more I spoke with French locals, the topic of Chablis and food came up time and time again. This is a go-to white wine for food in France. Champagne and Muscadet may be running a second and third, at least from my experience.

Chablis is made from Chardonnay, and has a little more of a new world taste to it compared to the other white burgundies. Chablis from Burgundy is typically made clean, devoid of the heavy over-oaking that you experience with so many of the California Chardonnay. Luckily, the over oaking seems to be a trend on the decline here which is good. When you try good clean Chardonnay, like that from Chablis, you can really get a taste for the grape, and the citrus, flowery freshness that can be subdued by oak aging.

Chablis remains an excellent white wine choice for almost any occasion and like many of the other great French wines, you are starting to see more and more bottles carried in the stores here in the US.

Burgundy Ratings

The top wines from Burgundy will hold one of two designations: 1) Grand Cru and 2) Premier Cru. Grand Cru typically means the wine is from the highest quality single vineyard, while Premier Cru means a high quality single vineyard. If you see those words on the bottle, you know you are in for a treat. "Village" is a third designation below the other two that means that it is a multiple vineyard wine.

Alsace

Alsace is a historic area tucked away in far eastern France on the border near Germany and Switzerland, northeast of Burgundy. You'll notice that some of the Alsatian wines will exhibit characteristics similar to that of neighboring Germany and their excellent Rieslings.

Wines from Alsace fall into two classifications, Alsace Grand Cru and Alsace AC. The Alsace Grand Cru is made from one of four grapes: Riesling, Muscat, Pinot Gris or Gewurztraminer. Regular Alsace wines also include Pinot Blanc and may be comprised of a blend of these grapes (which is quite common in many of the bottles I see).

Alsatian wines are usually aromatic and full in body while being a touch drier than their German counterparts, and devoid of heavy oak influencing. I find these wines to be excellent values, starting right in the $15-$20 range for excellent whites, and moving up from there.

Riesling and Gewurztraminer are varietals many US consumers find too sugary and sweet. I agree in large part but the wines from Alsace prove that the varietals can be made a little spicier and floral to open up some beautiful characteristics you wouldn't typically associate with these grapes. The only way to know if they work for you is to give them a try.

<u>Interesting note:</u> Alsace is the only appellation in France to produce wines labeled by varietal instead of region. So don't think you're buying an odd bottle if you see the varietals listed on the label, especially after reading this far and learning about every other wine being listed by region.

Southern France

Rhone Valley

The Rhone Valley in Southern France produces stellar wines using many different grapes than those found in other parts of France. In fact, in the popular and renowned Chateauneuf-du-Pape region, blends can utilize 13 different grapes. It sounds like it could get complicated but it really isn't. You just have to know a few basic fundamentals of the geography and you'll be on your way to enjoying these excellent Southern French wines.

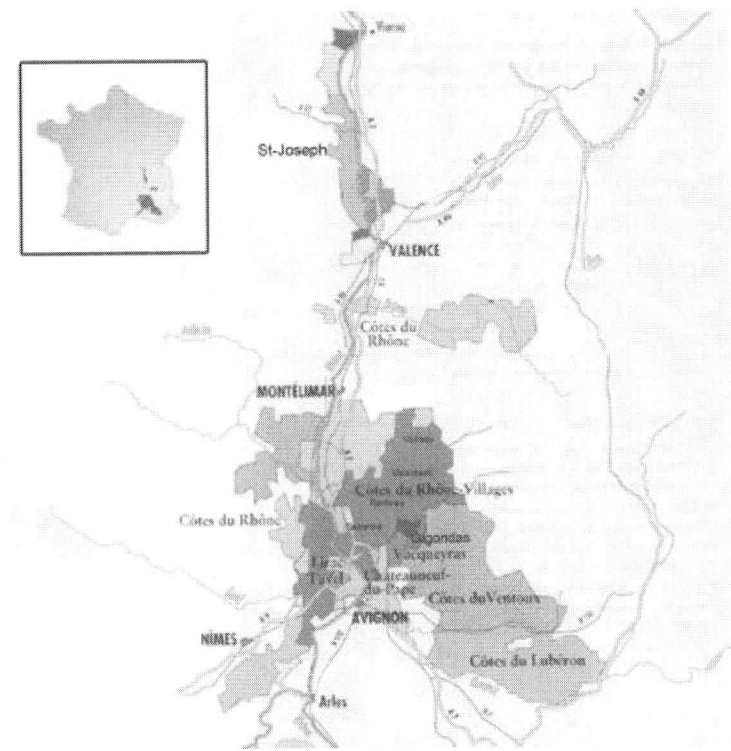

As I mentioned previously, I've developed a special interest in Rhone wines. They stand out to me because they exude the beauty of the French land, with old vine heritage, and they are consistently exceptional values from the low end ($10) all the way to the high end ($300+). I find them to be incredibly food friendly too.

Northern Rhone

Northern Rhone is noted for its Syrah which is the primary red grape that is grown in the area. Interestingly enough to many US wine consumers, the winemakers in Northern Rhone will blend their Syrah with small parts of white grapes, including Viognier, Marsanne and Roussanne. Fans of Australian wines may find that more familiar since you see that occur more frequently with Australian Shiraz.

A result of these blends is the growing international popularity of some of these Northern Rhone vineyards, particularly those from Cote Rotie and St Joseph. And unfortunately, prices are rising along with their popularity. But if you search around you can still find some of these great wines for $40-$50.

Some of the appellations of Northern Rhone to keep an eye out for are:

- Hermitage (highly regarded, must try region)

- Crozes-Hermitage

- Cote Rotie

- Saint Joseph

Fast Fact: Crozes-Hermitage is Northern Rhone's largest volume producer and the wines share many characteristics with Hermitage with a more approachable balance of flavor, and price tag.

Southern Rhone

Southern Rhone has a bit warmer climate than its neighbor to the north. In addition to Syrah, which is popular in the region, you will also see blends with Grenache (dominantly), Mourvedre, Cinsault and Carignan. These are the staples of what are known as "Rhone Varietals" which continue to grow in popularity around the world.

Today you will find a lot of these same grapes grown in South America, often times from vines brought over from France, and there's a strong emergence lately of the varietals in California. The acclaimed Chateau de Beaucastel of Chateauneuf-du-Pape offers their Tablas Creek wines grown in Paso Robles, and there's even an organization known as the "Rhone Rangers" who promote the growth and consumption of Rhone varietals. This is clearly an area at the center of the modern wine world.

Some of the key appellations in Southern Rhone that you will want to commit to memory include:

Cotes du Rhone: a staple of the area, lots of Grenache dominated blends and typically a safe bet at almost any price point. If you start dipping below $10 you'll be pushing it, but for just a few dollars more, $12-$15, you'll be right in the sweet spot. That said, when you go even further up market, in that $20-$30 range these wines are on par with bottles twice the price from other areas. (note: the prices I list may vary widely depending on where you are buying your wine. Please use this as just a rough guide for what to expect.)

Cotes du Rhone Villages: attached to the northern part of Cotes du Rhone. Comments from above apply here too.

Gigondas: a really fun region, and one that demands proper exploration. Bottles from Gigondas are typically right in that $20 range, and they are made with the Grenache Noir grape. Never tried it? Now's the time.

Cotes du Ventoux: this is an up and comer, at least to US markets. A couple years ago you'd be hard pressed to find many Ventoux bottles in your average wine shop. But they are creeping into a wine store near you, and they are a great representation of the values from this region.

<u>Vacqueyras</u>: Take it from me: You are safe buying almost any bottle that says Vacqueyras on it. To test this for my readers, I went out and scooped up one for $8 at Total Wine. It was one of the best $8 wines in recent memory. But to get a true taste for these wines, look to spend in the $15-$20 range. It will taste like it cost much more than that, I'm certain.

<u>Chateauneuf-du-Pape:</u> I shouldn't be bashful. Chateauneuf-du-Pape is hands down one of my favorite wine regions in the world. It began around a table at a French restaurant in Paris where I was hanging with some local hosts, who knew of my love for French wines. I was only mildly familiar with Chateauneuf at that time, and as the food was being ordered, the locals ordered a couple different Chateauneuf bottles. They told me they were going for the "local stuff," which after clarification they told me is the wine that is so good that the French don't ship it to the rest of the world. I'm sure there's a little truth to that. The wine they ordered was magnificent, and I scoured a few local markets the next day hoping to find some to take with me. I found some great wines, but to this day have never found the wines they ordered.

<u>Side note:</u> As I write this second edition of the book, I am drinking a Chateaufneuf to get in the spirit of the content. I am drinking the

2009 Les Vignes d'Alexandre Châteauneuf-du-Pape you see pictured here that I purchased for $40, and it is excellent at this price.

Rasteau: a sleeper from Rhone in my opinion. You don't see shelves stocked with Rasteau bottles, but I've had great experiences at the high and low end of this region too.

Costieres de Nimes: Like Ventoux, this is an up and comer. It's one of the newer regions to be classified as a Rhone wine. I've tried a few bottles, with mixed reviews to be honest. This is one to keep an eye on though.

The White Wines of Rhone

Like Bordeaux, Rhone is known for its reds, but that's not to say you won't find some fun white wines from this area. White wines will be blended too and may include grapes such as Viognier, Roussanne, Marsanne and Grenache Blanc along with some lesser known grapes such as Ugni Blanc, Bourboulenc, Picpoul, and Clairette. Chateauneuf-du-Pape produces excellent white wines (and Rose too) that can usually be purchased at a fair price.

Languedoc-Roussillon

Languedoc is a monster volume producer of some of France's best value wine, and at least up until recent years, produced more wine than the entire US. Languedoc shares many of the same climate and soil characteristics as neighboring Rhone, and the wines share similar attributes as well.

Note: GSM – a common term to describe a blend of Grenache, Syrah and Mourvedre.

Languedoc is home to other grape varietals as well including Cabernet Sauvignon, Cinsault and Merlot and even whites such Sauvignon Blanc and Chardonnay. Wines from Languedoc will come from a host of different geographical classifications including Corbieres, Faugeres, Minervois, Saint-Chinian and Roussillon, the latter of which you seem to see in more and more US stores and on restaurant wine lists.

Most of the GSM wines you will find will exhibit big jammy flavors with touches of black pepper and they can be drank young if you like them ripe and fruity, or wait a few years to let them settle and help the tannins to mature.

Champagne

"In victory you deserve Champagne. In defeat, you need it," -- Napoleon Bonaparte.

This is probably the most misunderstood region for French wine. For the average wine buyer, anything with bubbles is considered Champagne, which is as far from the truth as you can get. Champagne is an area of France, about 90 miles northeast of Paris, and the only "true Champagne" originates from here.

Quick Fact: The British were the first to create bottles that were strong enough to contain the pressure of effervescent wine, and the French were the first to use them commercially.

Wines from Champagne are typically made with Pinot Noir and Chardonnay and they carry with them designations such as Prestige Cuvee (the best from the winemaker), Blanc de noirs (made from red grapes, but still white, no skins), Blanc de blanc (made from Chardonnay), and Rose (some Pinot Noir used).

You'll see these designations on the label and they provide a guide for what to expect on the inside. Champagne has really gained in popularity in the US over the last few years since it complements just about any meal (not just a special occasion). It is also a perfect wine to bring to almost any dinner party or occasion where the host is a wine lover.

Serving Champagne: In the US, we usually drink our reds too warm, and our whites too cold. Champagne is one of those whites we typically chill too much. Ideal drinking temperature for Champagne is about 45 degrees Fahrenheit or 7 degrees Celsius which is much warmer than it will be straight out of the fridge. Either pull the bottle out 15 minutes before you plan to drink it, or do what the experts do and place it in a bottle that is half water and half ice. By getting the wine to be the proper temperature you will be able to taste the full spectrum of flavors that can be inhibited when the wine is too cold.

Or you can follow some advice straight from 007 *"My dear girl, there are some things that just aren't done, such as drinking Dom Perignon '53 above the temperature of 38 degrees Fahrenheit. That's just as bad as listening to the Beatles without earmuffs!"* – Sean Connery as James Bond in Goldfinger, 1964.

Let's Wrap This Up

I wrote this because it took me a long time to learn about each of these areas, to know what grapes are produced where, and to know what to expect so I can pair with food, or buy for the occasion. And I'm still going.

The experience of writing this has helped me learn something, and that is that my work is just beginning. I'm making a commitment to keep hitting new areas, and to learn more about Champagne which is growing in popularity perhaps more than ever before. I want to buy some bottles from Graves, keep going after those right bank Bordeaux, and stock up on the 2010 vintage. I also want to expand my experiences in Burgundy where the possibilities seem endless.

The wine rep whose story I opened with has proved to be right. It helps to focus on one area. I catch myself moving into Italian and Spanish wines and I start to feel the force sucking me into postponing my French wine studies to indulge in some of these other great European wines. There's just so much to learn and the wines from Italy and Spain are amazing too. But these dilemmas are what make wine exploration so fun. Adding to the excitement, new wines are produced every year and they can be a little bit different, reminding me that this game isn't going to end for a long time.

I hope you enjoyed reading this, and always remember "La vie est trop courte pour boire du mauvais vin."

Andrew Cullen, acullen@gmail.com

If you enjoyed this short book and wish to explore the wine world beyond France, please check out my latest wine book now available in paperback and Kindle formats on Amazon.com: *Around the Wine World in 40 Pages: An Exploration Guide for the Beginning Wine Enthusiast.*

FRENCH WINE TASTING MENU WITH SUGGESTED PAIRINGS

Here's a quick reference menu that you can use as a guide to exploring some of the wines mentioned in this book, as well as food that would pair nicely with them. Use this as a fun way to "check off" wines and regions as you explore them, or even as a guide to throwing a French Wine tasting party.

- Bordeaux Pauillac (Red): Red meat, game, all steaks, strong cheese
- Bordeaux Margaux (Red): Red meat, game, all steaks, strong cheese
- Bordeaux Pomerol (Red): Mild red meat, stews, roast duck
- Bordeaux St Emilion (Red): Mild red meat, stews, roast duck
- Graves Pessac-Leognan (Red): Red meat, steak
- Graves Sauternes (White): Chocolates, pies, fruit tarts
- Burgundy Cote de Nuits (Red): Salmon, tuna, duck, pork, veal
- Burgundy Cote de Beaune (Red): Salmon, tuna, duck, pork, veal
- Burgundy Beaujolais (Red): Sweet pork, spicy poultry
- Burgundy Chablis (White): Crab, lobster, light fish, chicken, turkey

- Rhone Cote Rotie (Red): Pork, braised lamb shanks, beef fillet
- Rhone Cotes du Rhone (Red): Pork chops, chicken stir fry, roast turkey
- Rhone Chateauneuf-du-pape (Red): Spicy pork, beef
- Rhone Chateauneuf-du-pape (White): Seared tuna, grilled fish

ABOUT THE AUTHOR

Andrew Cullen is the author of "Decoding French Wine: A Beginner's Guide to Enjoying the Fruits of the French Terroir," "Around the Wine World in 40 Pages: An Exploration Guide for the Beginning Wine Enthusiast" and "New Customers Now: Using the Web's Best Free Tools to Market Your Small Business." He is a digital marketer for a global 100 brand and the founder of the websites www.CostcoWineBlog.com and www.ToysBulletin.com.

Made in the USA
San Bernardino, CA
15 September 2014